I0892329

MILL REEF STYLE

MILL REEF STYLE

THE MID-CENTURY MODERN ARCHITECTURE OF ROBERTSON WARD

TEXT BY ELIZABETH BALLANTINE AND STEPHEN S. LASH

PHOTOGRAPHS BY RICHARD CHEEK

THE DERRYDALE PRESS Lanham, Maryland • New York • Plymouth, U.K.

MILL REEF
CORK POINT
GREEN ISLAND
Isiri
Nonsuch Bay
Onesuch
Fort Harman
Ten Pound Bay
Rickett's Bay
Moongate
NECK OF LAND
Bamboo
Little Deep Bay
Aquamarine
Great Deep Bay
YORK ISLAND
WICKED WILL
ANTIGUA
Marigalante Bay
Friar's Head
Point of View
Exchange Bay
Clubhouse
Bali Li
Signal Point
SMITH ISLAND
Half Moon Bay

Introduction 7

11 The Vision of Happy Ward

Clubhouse 26

38 Bali Li

Fort Harman 46

54 Friar's Head

Signal Point 62

74 Aquamarine

Bamboo 84

92 Point of View

Moongate 100

110 Onesuch

Isiri 118

127 Selected Works of Robertson Ward

Introduction

The magic of the Mill Reef Club first appears when the taxi carrying tired travelers suddenly twists left down the ridge from Willoughby Bay. The incomparable view of Half Moon Bay, Exchange Bay, Smith and York islands, the shining bits of houses in the low scrubby vegetation, the white cupola on Friar's Head: all stretch in the distance. This magnificent panorama never fails to cause a rush of excitement.

The view has changed little in the more than sixty years that have passed since the club opened, in 1949.

In 2002, a few years after the club's golden anniversary celebration, Stephen Lash and I discussed the importance of an inventory of the Mill Reef houses built by Robertson (Happy) Ward (1897–1988). Even though the landscape and the number of houses at Mill Reef remained, changes in construction materials, water supply, aesthetic fashions, and technologies were eroding their original architecture and that of the clubhouse. We believed that Ward's original vision, with its focus on local materials and craftsmen and simple but very stylish houses, should be explored and elucidated for the benefit of future generations of homeowners and club members. In fact, the "green" aspects of Ward's architecture, based on use of rainwater, close attention to ocean breezes, and an open embrace of surrounding landscape and gardens, are very timely concepts today.

To give these thoughts concrete visual expression, our friend S. Allen Chambers, Jr., author and senior architectural historian of the Historic American Buildings Survey at the U.S. Department of the Interior, recommended the well-known Boston-based architectural and landscape photographer Richard Cheek. Richard has created color portrait books for such august institutions as the Garden Club of Virginia, The Trustees of Reservations in Massachusetts, and Old Westbury Gardens on Long Island; has taken photographs for dozens of architectural guides and histories; and has generally had the privilege of documenting some of America's most famous buildings, from the White House and the Breakers to the Beinecke Library and H. H. Richardson's Trinity Church. We invited Richard to visit the club, plied him with rum punch, and asked him to take on the job of photographing the remaining original houses and the clubhouse at Mill Reef.

In five visits over several years, in varied conditions and seasons, Richard completed that assignment. Stephen and I observed him, time and again, spending hours in splendid solitude waiting for just the right light patterns on cement walls or shadows cast by palm fronds, insisting on capturing illustrative shots. We saw another artistic temperament attuned to Happy Ward's vision.

Richard's photos outperformed the basic task: to record the Mill Reef Club properties and landscape, the ocean, the offshore islands, and the skies of the eastern side of Antigua. His pictures bring us far more than documentation or the simple record of a time and place. Richard's camera illuminates the high drama of the setting of the tropics, the showy magnificence of the light and shadows of clouds, the ever-changing blues and movement of the sea. Richard shows us that Ward's architecture embraces nature with rooms open to the outdoors and that his structures rise and fall with changes in elevation of the landscape. The viewer smoothly

The view across Rickett's Bay to Fort Harman, with Neck of Land in the distance.

follows the passage from interior to exterior, shares a sense of delight at a panoramic view or a quick glimpse of the sea. Everything is dynamic: the clouds, the water, the omnipresent wind bending the trees and vegetation, the movement from room to room, from corridor to corridor, in and out of a house. We see Happy Ward's architecture and the dreams of his clients more profoundly through the lens of Richard's camera than with the naked eye.

As Stephen writes in his essay, the concept of building at Mill Reef was to be modest and understated for the times. (The original cost of the houses was to be no more than $25,000, it was later raised to $40,000.) But the lifestyle of the original members was lavish and embraced much artificiality. Bamboo, the home of Elsa Mott Mitchell Ives, most evidently expresses this. The use of bamboo throughout the house, the extension of the coral reef rising under the dining room table, the perfect "rat pack" feeling of the built-in bar—all of these aspects (and many others) were devised to bring people together for frivolous fun and high style. This house evokes Hollywood of the 1950s. Bali Li, Happy Ward's house, with its Balinese theme, offers a dining room table on stage, signifying the creative moment of dining and conversing together. This architecture was not for hermits! It was self-conscious and aware, with many literary and cultural references. It also reflects a highly orchestrated life of community exchange and socializing among the denizens of the many houses and the clubhouse.

Ward paid attention to decorative details in his houses because he had to. In the early years, he and his stepson, Amos Morrill, were doing it all: mixing paint, building furniture, and sculpting cement dolphins for a fountain as well as planning cisterns and plumbing. Everything had to be done on the spot and with local materials. Richard captures this creativity: a cistern takes the shape of a windmill (Onesuch), front doors open to outdoor views (Exchange Bay), cement floors are tinted red and scratched with designs (Bamboo, Aquamarine, Signal Point), and gun embrasures become windows (Fort Harman).

Islands notably have always attracted immigrants of many races and origins; in the case of Antigua, not only Africans of diverse regions and British colonial rulers but also Lebanese, Syrians, Asians, Indians, Irish, and North and South Americans. Ward's houses capitalized on a wide range of sources: Native American pueblos, Hong Kong, windmills, military fortresses, British Georgian manors. Surprising today, the Ward cement houses forgo indigenous Caribbean or Arawak wood building styles. The theme of a transitory visitor observing the dramatic landscape is very clear in Richard Cheek's pictures. Although the images are empty of people, the viewer sees them in his mind's eye. Note, for example, the wide-angle photo that opens this book, showing empty chairs facing Marigalante Bay on the Friar's Head terrace. The sounds of laughter and animated conversation waft through the viewer's consciousness as imaginary vacationers marvel at the changing colors of water, sky, and clouds.

The houses we selected for Richard's work are a mixture that is partly accidental. It depended on which owners were amenable to invasion by a photographer at a given time, which photos turned out depending on the weather and other factors, and which houses had been maintained well enough over the decades to preserve original built-in furniture and decorative features. A number of Mill Reef houses were neglected and passed through absentee owners. Although the focus here is on the clubhouse and ten mostly original houses (there are others), photos of architectural details and scenic views come from many other properties as well.

What *is* a Happy Ward house at Mill Reef? In essence, it is a cement habitation built over or near a water cistern and catchments. It comprises two (or three) bedrooms, flat or shallow roofs, a living room open to the west, a walk-in bar near the front door (stocked with the owner's special rum punch), and an indoor plant room or garden with a fish or lily pond or other water feature. All the houses have most of these features, unless the location on a point or promontory is too exposed.

The houses are identified here by their original names. Nearly all houses at Mill Reef have been expanded or remodeled but still reflect the original scale and concepts. Andrew Goodenough, a British architect trained in London, who in 1980 at age twenty-nine opened a practice in English Harbour (several miles southwest of Mill Reef and a popular tourist destination), has performed the giant share of this work. In most cases, he has expanded the living space but broken it down into separate buildings and rooflines. A good example of his work is Point of View, designed in the 1950s by Ward in an angular modernist style with abutting window casements. In 1999, Goodenough expanded the living room, added wooden pergolas to increase the shaded area on the terrace, and designed the swimming pool and pool pavilion. (Due to scarce rainfall and before the government installed a desalination plant, swimming pools were rare at Mill Reef.)

The clubhouse has been altered numerous times, from small expansions of administrative spaces over the decades to large renovations financed by members in the 1990s. The dining room (with its dance floor that doubles as a water catchment), the bar, and the two floors of now expanded club rooms are the remaining original parts. In 1981, Ward constructed the Ward Room, an expansion off the dining room for a card and game area. As part of a major updating and remodeling in the late 1990s, Andrew converted many of the small twin-bedded rooms to suites, added rooms in the empty space between the two original blocks of rooms, and added or expanded cottages. This upgrade took place over several years, replacing the spartan (and deteriorating) small rooms with expansive, modern spaces. Richard's photos focus on the public rooms and corridors.

Mechanical upgrades such as air-conditioning and TV are still extremely rare at Mill Reef houses. Handwritten messages are placed in members' and visitors' mailboxes at the club to provide communication. (The introduction of Wi-Fi is changing some of this custom.) But trade winds still cool the clubhouse bedrooms, and public spaces and cisterns still supply some of the water for human consumption.

Ward designed nearly all of the fifty-five houses at Mill Reef. The vast majority were built in the 1950s. In addition, he constructed nearly all the hotels built in that time on Antigua, launching the Antiguan resort industry (including the Curtain Bluff and Half Moon Bay hotels—the latter destroyed by a hurricane in 1995. Although Ward continued to spend time at Mill Reef with friends and clients, he sold his house in 1965 to focus on other opportunities in the Caribbean and around the world. By then he had built two of his best known projects, Sandy Lane hotel in Barbados (1961) and Cotton Bay Club in Eleuthera (1962).

Stephen, whose career as an executive of Christie's has allowed him to observe many patrons and their architectural styles, is well qualified to assess the architecture of Happy Ward. Stephen and his wife, Wendy, first visited Mill Reef in 1967 and have returned every year since. He analyzes Ward's architectural style in the context of expanding international travel after World War II. Following the prewar discovery of Florida as a vacation paradise reachable by train, people now were eager to travel by plane in search of more exotic diversions and faraway cultures. Since then, four generations of visitors and members have followed the early travelers who discovered the breezes and bluffs of Mill Reef.

We have included on page 127 a partial list of Ward's projects based on documents at the American Institute of Architects in Washington, D.C., that were assembled in support of the lifetime achievement award he received from that organization in 1986. The construction dates and details cited in this book come mainly from those records, as well as from memoirs, popular lifestyle magazines, and the anecdotal accounts of club members at the time. The floor plans of the clubhouse and houses were drawn by Andrew Goodenough to reflect their present-day layout.

We thank the homeowners and Mill Reef Club members who supported this project as well as the employees who recalled for us the early members and construction of houses. Andrew Goodenough patiently led us amateurs through the details of his work and its intersection with that of Happy Ward. We are grateful to the late Morley Ballantine, Margot and Henry Bodmer, Don and Rosalie Culver, Pam and the late Jim Dana, Stewart Dansby, Ruth and Bruce Dayton, Helen and Ed Healy, Wendy Lash, Christine Layng, Paul Leavitt, Ernie and Catriona Letby, Bona Macy, Allen and Musette Morgan, Barrie Pickering, Tina Rathborne and Philip deNormandie, Kathleen Walker, Claire and Brad Wheatley, and George Yeager.

We especially thank Al Chambers for his invaluable counsel and enthusiasm. Without him we never would have completed our earlier work, *A Vision of Paradise: Robertson Ward and the Mill Reef Club*, published in 2001, nor this book. Many thanks also go to Richard Cheek, designer Julia Sedykh, and editors Giselle Minoli, James Mooney, and Chase Olivarius-McAllister.

Finally, we are very grateful to all the homeowners who have acted as stewards of Mill Reef and its architectural traditions.

We hope this second volume will acquaint members with new aspects of the club and its heritage that they will be inspired to honor and preserve.

—Elizabeth Ballantine

The Vision of Happy Ward

In 1946, the modernist architect Robertson (Happy) Ward envisioned and began to design and build the Mill Reef Club on Antigua, West Indies. During the early postwar years, other Caribbean clubs were founded and many foundered. Yet in the dozen years following 1946, Mill Reef not only survived but also thrived and managed to earn and bask in public acclaim. In a 1958 feature on the Caribbean, *Newsweek* reported that "there is no doubt that the brightest leisure-time jewel in the West Indies today is the Mill Reef Club on Antigua." The club was founded "after World War II by a group of congenial, well-to-do, and in some cases retired Americans." Their "common aim" was to find "some part of the West Indies that would furnish a suitable location for a club." *Newsweek* further noted: "Led by architect Robertson (Happy) Ward, they sought their goal in businesslike fashion, evaluating all the islands on a point system, weighing them on climate, accessibility, political stability, and physical character of the land."[1]

Ward's unpublished memoir belies a less precise approach to this search for the ideal domain of a members-only club. On first surveying a beguiling and bashful Antigua—after an exhaustive tour of the more obvious Caribbean islands—Ward found his paradise. "I immediately exclaimed that this was it!"[2] However the choice of locale was made, it was auspicious: Antigua, certainly, is the rock on which the club's success has relied. Yet the December 1976 issue of *Town & Country* argued that Antigua was the chief beneficiary of Ward's vision for Mill Reef. According to the magazine, the island's first piece of luck was the restoration of English Harbour, its eighteenth-century British naval station once commanded by Vice Admiral Horatio Lord Nelson. "The other," said *Town & Country*, "was the creation of Mill Reef." The same article noted that the club "which detests being referred to as a millionaire's enclave—is a tightly screened social outpost dedicated to inconspicuous good living for America's Old Guard and power elite," the "end-all of prestigious residential clubs," and "the creation of Robertson 'Happy' Ward, that peripatetic American architect who catalyzed most of the early rush to the tropics."[3]

From the first, Ward's vision was as sociological as it was architectural. All architecture is social engineering. Ward was determined to engineer a society in which pretension was absent, nature was undeniable, and pleasure was infinite.

It takes half a century or more to assess properly the legacy of an architect. Lifestyles, the evolving role of the family, conveniences, communication options, transportation, and much else change in the decades after the architect first approaches the drawing board. Indeed, appreciating Ward's vision is impossible without locating it in the wider history of American postwar travel, members' clubs, and modernist architecture.

Travel

"In the cool of the evening we were perfectly enraptured with the beautiful prospects which every side presented to our view—the field of cane, corn, fruit trees & in a delightful green." So wrote a young Virginian of good family during a vacation to Barbados in 1751. His name was George Washington, and in addition to being

The mid-century modern louvered corner window is a signature Happy Ward feature, appearing in many of the homes he designed. This view encompasses not only Exchange Bay but also the houses called Exchange Place, Bali Li, and Friar's Head.

the future Father of his Country, it now turns out, he was fathering another trend—the annual exodus of distinguished Americans to the southernmost islands of the Caribbean.

—*Newsweek*, 1958[4]

Ever since George Washington returned safely from Barbados, Americans have been fascinated with the Caribbean, regardless of the difficulties involved in getting there. When *Holiday* magazine was revived in 1946 by the Curtis Publishing Company, its editor, Ted Patrick, wrote in the September issue about the complications of travel:

> You have the money to spend, the desire to go, and the welcome awaiting you.
>
> But, when you decide to turn your urge into actual travel, you find yourself fettered in passport and visa paperwork so irritating and exhausting that you're almost willing to settle for a canoe trip, bike ride, or holiday at home with a good book.
>
> Many of the procedures involving visas, health certificates, police certificates, permits, photographs, cash deposits, were necessary during wartime. But there is a persistent rumor that the war is over. The time has come to take the legalistic pain out of touring for business or pleasure.[5]

The war was over. A desire for travel beckoned. This is what sets Patrick's account of traveling apart from Washington's, which consisted of unabashed pleasure, and from that of the 1946 traveler, which speaks of unremitting inconvenience. The kind of traveling that Patrick envisioned for his readers and fellow citizens was the meeting of a personal longing; it was also many other things. Patrick exhorted readers to travel in spite of the inconveniences because "this is the first peacetime summer, the first whole year of silent guns." We need to make and keep ourselves happy and healthy by traveling, he wrote:

> *Holiday* is dedicated to the pursuit of happiness. For all those who see "go" signs on the horizon, for all those who seek to get more sheer living of life itself, *Holiday* is created. . . . *Holiday* is designed for this new postwar world, a world in which recreation will be more important to everyone than ever before—more important in this busier world of new stresses and strains because more and more doctors are prescribing escape, and travel, and fun.[6]

Yet mid-century Americans feared air travel. An article entitled "They Make Air Travel Safer" talked about "enlisting radar to conquer the hazards of bad weather," alongside advertisements for Airlite Luggage and the rayon-wool blend of Kohinoor Sportswear (which recommended itself as being particularly congenial to air travelers). The mid-century tourist craved exposure to foreign lands, an experience that only travel could produce. Yet that tourist was also terrified of what boarding a flight might mean in terms of his bodily safety, attire, comfort, existential well-being, and of what being American might signify elsewhere—and might ever afterward signify to him.

One of the Mill Reef Club's first members, the celebrated poet and playwright Archibald MacLeish, articulated Americans' hankering for escape, and he addressed the effects of the war on American travelers in an elegiac preface to his 1953 radio play, *This Music Crept by Me upon the Waters*:

> It is a voyage many Americans made, intentionally or unintentionally, in years between the two world wars when Pan Am's flying boats began to follow the sickle curve of the Antilles through the Leeward Islands and the Windwards.
>
> It did not last long, that brief world of Far. After the Second World War its sky was webbed with the contrails of enormous jets and every cove had two hotels at least and you could telephone New York from anywhere. But for a few years, till that happened, men and women, playing at the living of their lives, sometimes almost found them in that wind, that moon.[7]

These lines become more poignant when one considers that this play was written at Mill Reef and recounts a dinner party there. The characters are transformed by the drama of the setting sun and the rising moon.

MacLeish's eulogy for the "brief world of Far" that Americans sought in the period between the two world wars is passionate and, like all exercises in true nostalgia, painful to read. It was a world a heartfelt, inquisitive, and ultimately patriotic fantasy—that Americans, like George Washington before them, could inhabit by voyaging to the Caribbean. The fact that World War II destroyed

Less than a year after the end of the war, *Holiday* magazine appeared with Pan Am advertisements celebrating the allure of travel and depicting "a world of neighbors" in comfortable and luxurious aircraft such as the Stratocruiser—replaced in recent years by the 747 and A380.

An Antiguan sugar mill survives at the entrance to the club, evocative of the structures that dot the landscape of the island. It is impossible to disassociate Antigua from its roots in the sugar trade that date back to the seventeenth century.

The club's logo as it appears at the entrance gate, surmounted by a miniature concrete windmill. The club name is framed in a classic border above the triple-wave motif.

The flag of the island and the burgee of the club appear prominently at the entrance.

that dream makes MacLeish's imagination of travel all the more vivid and internally alive. Yet the war did not kill Americans' desire for escape and travel. If anything, the end of the war rejuvenated it. MacLeish had been speaking to a loss: the impossibility of travel sating the American soul in a postwar world in which all was convenient, known, and unromantically proximate. Today, second and third homes are commonplace. Hotels—many built on a huge scale—condominiums, cooperative apartments, time-shares, and retirement communities populate the Caribbean. Flights are more affordable, and Americans fly abroad in greater numbers than even *Holiday* or MacLeish could have anticipated.

But in another more complicated and truer sense, history has also redeemed MacLeish's view: the ease of modern travel in part means that nothing is truly far away. The "brief world of Far" is indeed over. Ward understood how to preserve that world, with architecture that would enliven and guarantee community within a beautifully isolated enclave. Perhaps it is over for the vast majority of American tourists, who do not belong to the Mill Reef Club.

Social Environment

Antigua may be the basic source of the Mill Reef Club's success, but the club's great attraction cannot be attributed solely to the island. Although the club was enticingly far away, the social principle on which it was organized was close to home: exclusivity.

Happy Ward's own social outlook was informed and shaped by his eclectic background. He was a gentleman, sportsman, artist, gardener, inveterate traveler, and, tellingly, the out-of-wedlock child of Frederick William MacMonnies, the distinguished yet controversial expatriate American sculptor. (Ward long maintained the family cover story—necessary in that era—that his mother had briefly been married to an American businessman in Italy, John Robertson Ward, who died shortly after young Robertson's birth.) Another expatriate forebear on his mother's side was the famed eighteenth-century American painter Benjamin West. Ward arrived on the scene in Antigua in 1946, equipped not only with a high quotient of intelligence but also with extensive experience, endless curiosity, and that eclectic background.

Clearly his plan for Mill Reef was a very personal one, the musings of a peripatetic young man who only learned of his true parentage when he met his father for the first time, as an adult. A "club" implies collegiality and shared values but seldom implies "diversity." It may very well have been that inclusiveness was important to Ward because he was not part of the most basic community that many take for granted: the family. Although he made a gesture toward diverse membership from the beginning through the recruitment of foreign members and people from the Midwest, nearly all offshore members were white Anglo-Saxon Protestants. The introduction of diversity came later, with membership invitations extended to prominent Antiguans, including black leaders and various heads of government.

Although it would change over time, in the early years this newly created "community" did not become family-centered or diverse. It was still an era when children were "seen, not heard," if not altogether left at home. Geographical differences apart, there was no real diversity at the club. It was a social class that included few Jews, few Catholics—mainly WASPs, and many from Yale at that. There was a centrality to club life, entertainment, and recreation that revolved around friendship more than around family.

There was something exciting about traveling a great distance to break free of postwar constraints, to escape frigid winters and free oneself from the economic shackles of a less comfortable postwar world. Not only were servants in short supply, increasingly expensive and anachronistic at home, but there was also a kind of social breakdown in which any previously assumed societal order was no longer assured. The decidedly different fast-track of the postwar world made the social order of a cosseted club even more enticing, for it would provide a welcome relief from the realities of life and a fantasy return, however brief, to prewar leisure.

Moreover, the vision of Happy Ward was part of a larger vision of clubs, hotels, and resorts that could respond to the demands of the newly prosperous and frenzied postwar world. This period also saw the emergence of other clubs, such as Coral Beach in Bermuda and Cotton Bay in Eleuthera. Hotels such as the RockResorts of the 1950s—Caneel Bay, Little Dix, Dorado Beach, and Mauna Kea—reflected a similar taste for a conservation-minded utopia in which the profit motive was long-term and underplayed. Although several of these establishments survive, others have moved in new directions. Dorado Beach has been leveled, Coral Beach awaits the plans of a real estate developer, and while Cotton Bay is no longer a club it is likely to be revived in some form.

Today, club members continue to endorse Ward's core belief that Mill Reef must moderate real estate inflation if it is to stay true to its social and cultural mission. House prices are effectively held down by a controlled market that both prevents substantial profit-taking when property is sold or transferred and encourages purchases by new owners. Mortgages are not permitted. In addition, mass-market development has been slow to reach Antigua, which is still a relatively remote and small (108 square miles) island that presents itself as an upscale resort.

Mill Reef differentiates itself with its style, which is the product of understatement, resourcefulness, and mid-century modern building designs suited to the environment of the Caribbean and the sophisticated tastes of a well-educated, well-traveled, accomplished, and privileged population. Of course, early members' desires to join the Mill Reef Club were complicated. Some in the American set savored the company of expatriate British colonials, whose rakish charms were difficult to resist. For other members, a move to Antigua was an economic decision spurred by a desire to hang on to a lifestyle that could no longer be maintained at home. Also underpinning Ward's concept was the idea that a winter getaway in the Caribbean was not an outrageous luxury but something within the reach of genteel folk who were merely comfortable rather than rich. There were also far fewer travel options than there are today, and the Caribbean offered reasonable access to virgin territory while other destinations were geographically distant and only slowly recovering from the ravages of war.

Although the club today has significantly more creature comforts and is more democratic and diverse, the world outside has not remained the same. Antigua has evolved from an impoverished dependency of the British empire to an independent Commonwealth country, its politics dominated for decades by the Bird family and a two-party, bitterly divided Labor oligarchy. It belongs to a global economy and imports workers from nearby islands and various countries. (Even the Chinese send laborers to Antigua.) Many Antiguans hold dual citizenship and live and work seasonally in a second country, chiefly the U.K. or the United States. Posh resorts charge winter rates of more than $5,000 per night and are sold out during the gold-plated Christmas-holiday season. Mill Reef, blessed with abundant land acquired in another era and strict rules against land speculation, remains an oasis of splendid retreat for its high-minded and tightly screened members and guests.

Architecture

Ward's architectural designs reflected a simplicity and understatement that were the by-products of the social, economic, and environmental realities of launching a real estate development in the Caribbean in the immediate postwar years. Simplicity and a connection to the natural environment ruled, and since most houses had no more than one guest bedroom, nonproprietary members (that is, those without their own homes) and guests had to rely on club accommodations.

Unlike Le Corbusier in France and Ludwig Mies van der Rohe and Walter Gropius in Germany, Ward rejected the belief that modernist architecture transcended all—history, nationality, locality. His modernist architecture capitalized on geographic and cultural influences. In fact, he demonstrated a distinctly non-modernist inclination toward fantasy in decoration and embellishments at Mill Reef. The result was a cocktail of influences. The original Sandy Lane hotel, designed by Ward in Barbados in 1962, was "influential in marrying the finest traditions of Palladianism with Barbadian vernacular, and elevating Barbadian coral stone to almost the status of Italian marble!"[8] In Antigua, Ward exploited the same abundant native limestone and skills of local stonemasons to create the walls and arches and staircases of Mill Reef (without any machinery but by hand!).

Ward's taste was reflected not only in the design but also in the names of the exotic winter-vacation houses on Antigua. He named his own house Bali Li and filled it with Balinese architectural fragments and filigree. Conceived in the wake of the war, the house provided a joyful connection with a part of the world known during the war far less joyfully as the "Pacific Theater." This stylistic conceit is an example of Ward's delight in juxtaposing the old and the new, the exotic and the mundane, the historic and the modern.

Perhaps Ward as architect, or Marjorie Lloyd-Smith as patron, chose to build Signal Point, a Moorish fortress enclosed by crenellated walls on a promontory separating Half Moon Bay from Exchange Bay. Hong Kong entered the tropics in Ward's evocation of a Chinese house and garden, appropriately named Moongate after the design of its entranceway—another Ward conceit that was later expanded upon in Andrew Goodenough's redesign.

Bert and Polly Work were among Mill Reef's pioneers. They did not begin their Antigua life in the grand house named Fort Harman (after the eponymous eighteenth-century edifice) but rather in their frame guesthouse, with its nineteenth-century fretwork and curlicue designs, characteristic of the eastern Caribbean.

The postwar world rediscovered China and introduced architectural elements such as the moon gate, a feature popular in Bermuda and replicated in redesigns of this Mill Reef house, the aptly named Moongate.

A blue and gold Thai temple-like ceiling shades the Bali Li terrace.

The saltwater swimming pool at Fort Harman boasts a fish eye that doubles as a stylish conversation area.

The entrance was an important feature of Ward's architecture, often incorporating gardens and descending stairways. Indoor garden rooms or slat houses provided protected spaces for tropical plants.

Ward's search for the exotic represented a variation on the theme of "escape," which was central to those first postwar issues of *Holiday* magazine. The subtext was clearly a sense of the "romance" associated with Ward's designs for other houses at Mill Reef. He played very well to the romantic motif in designing Friar's Head, an ersatz lighthouse named for the Atlantic-facing bluff of land on which it stands, a spot where an actual lighthouse might well have been a boon to sailors.

Adding to these themes of the romantic and the exotic, Archibald MacLeish introduced elements of irony and humor when he named his own simple house La Désirade after the small island off Guadeloupe that was discovered by Columbus and later became—of all things—the base for a leper colony. MacLeish wrote to Paul Buck, provost of Harvard University and his employer, on March 14, 1952: "You can't go far on an island seventeen miles across. Particularly when everything you want is at home. Columbus's La Désirade may be a leper colony but ours isn't."

MacLeish described his Mill Reef retreat:

> Cinder block house with a living room and two bedrooms on top of lime rock fifteen feet above and fifteen feet back from the clearest water a man could hope to find—shallow green-blue over coral reefs that run out a hundred yards to a deep blue channel with a little parched olive-green island beyond and the whole Atlantic over its shoulder. I work in a one room shack back up the hill.[9]

Were you Bert and Polly Work, who accompanied Ward on his early foray into the Caribbean, your shelter would have been the ruin of a recycled eighteenth-century fort named Harman where Happy Ward first built a small guesthouse, complete with Victorian fretwork. This provided the Works with temporary accommodations before building a serious house. "Adaptive reuse" was not a new concept to Ward, as evidenced by the mill he converted into a residence in New Canaan, Connecticut, in the early 1930s.[10] The original Fort Harman guesthouse survives today, and it has been sensitively replicated with the addition of a twin. Ward, incidentally, returned to the site in 1980 to add a pool in the shape of a fish, ushering in yet another era of family houses complete with swimming pools, despite the early persistent shortage of water in eastern Antigua—now remedied by a desalination plant.

For some, the appeal of escaping to these houses predated the war and might have been nurtured during the Depression years, when Hollywood films presented fantasies of an elegant, carefree, glamorous, and even theatrical world populated by characters played by the likes of Noel Coward, Fred Astaire, Ginger Rogers, and Marlene Dietrich. Such appears to have been the context in which postwar Bamboo was built for General Motors heiress Elsa Mott Mitchell Ives. There, Hollywood hit the tropics with a ramped-up dash of the exotic, provided by mirrors, silvered surfaces, and bamboo architectural accents in the bar, room partitions, furniture, structural supports, and on a thatched beach hut. So successful was this experiment that Bamboo was later incorporated into the renovation of Aquamarine, on adjacent Great Deep Bay.

The five miles of endlessly appealing beaches at Mill Reef, ranging from quiet waters to lively surf, also influenced the design of many of the residences. The houses along Great Deep and Little Deep bays, for example, are reminiscent of Frank Lloyd Wright's low-slung prairie houses. Ward's motivations were both aesthetic and practical. Architecturally, the lines of these houses reinforce the horizontality of the beach. The natural landscape was king, so Ward kept the houses low to the ground. Comfort, style, elegance, and simplicity prevailed without arrogantly trying to compete with nature. It is in this context that we appreciate houses and other beachfront retreats, which Ward sensitively managed to hide from the curious eyes of beach strollers with the clever use of foliage (all beaches on Antigua are public), while preserving the views from the houses toward the ocean.

The architecture of Mill Reef was also driven by necessity—by a shortage of water, intermittent electricity, no telephones, irregular air service, isolation, and generally insufficient supplies. It was underpinned by a respect for simplicity honed by Ward's upbringing and by a resourcefulness that may have been imposed by a postwar shortage of materials but that was also impelled by a sense of place that resulted in low-lying buildings resting comfortably in the landscape. "Green" architecture implies a healthy respect for the environment. Ward was really a "green architect" more out of necessity than ideals, although he was clearly forward-thinking, practical, innovative, and thrifty. The connection between architecture and landscape is observed at Friar's Head, where Ward experimented with an extraordinary and challenging site; it is further developed and refined at Isiri, with a series of pavilions hugging a hillside descending to the sea in rhythmic order.

The Legacy of Happy Ward

It was the compelling and captivating natural environment of Antigua that had captured Ward's imagination and continues to do so with visitors today. This experienced architect understood the importance of "location, location, location!" He was attracted to the drama of the landscape, coral outcroppings abutting azure seas, hillsides of lush vegetation punctuated with rustling majestic palms, open savannahs that remind one of now-abandoned fields of sugar cane, and vistas of the sea from every conceivable angle—on high, on low, nearby, and distant.

Ward was ahead of his time. His architecture was distinguished by its place in the landscape, by siting houses to capture not only the exciting vistas but also the wonderful breezes that are characteristic of the eastern end of Antigua. It is significant that even with the luxury of Mill Reef houses today there is little air-conditioning. Ward was careful to co-opt the natural environment in his architecture, bringing nature inside through the use of internal gardens and orchid rooms and using plantings of bougainvillea in many shades of red, orange, yellow, and white, plumbago in soft blue, and majestic pink and white oleander. He learned early that the planting of trees, bushes, and many flowers greatly enhanced the setting. Many of his houses are entered through garden forecourts, the architectural prelude to indoor entertainment spaces.

Ward's architecture was a mixture of practicality with flourishes of chic and style. It was prudent in a land of tropical storms to build structures into the lee of the hill. This was accomplished with siting that took advantage of magnificent views and trade winds, using architecture to frame and tame the landscape through the incorporation of classical ornament and traditional design vocabulary. The playful sense of theater that marks Mill Reef is evidenced by the approach to the club's entrance gate, through portals surmounted by windmill finials, and to its Beach Bar, through portals topped by pineapple finials. The descent to the beach from the clubhouse is by way of a steep, elegant staircase, made of local limestone, from which to preview the glorious pink sand, azure sea, and parade of stately palms directly below. Ward's theatrical architectural vocabulary repeats itself in other stairways and in gracious archways that descend to corridors of neatly hand-cut limestone blocks.

With its blend of formality and informality, Mill Reef reflects traditional architecture and traditional values. Many houses include formal dining rooms, several have libraries, and some have fireplaces—unexpected conceits on a tropical island. Early members of the club, many of them born before World War I and accustomed to having household help, adopted the etiquette of the British, who then still ruled Antigua.

Ward also had a gift for investing the utilitarian with flair. The dance floor adjoining the dining area of the clubhouse is actually a water catchment, with a cistern below. Elsewhere, the cistern took on the shape of a windmill, and an interior garden entrance was built over a major catchment. Such elements reflect the concern for conserving water in the club's early years on this arid island.

Ward's imagination was active not only about major issues but also about minor ones. Mies van der Rohe said, "God is in the details," and Ward understood that. He commissioned local craftsmen, of whom there were many at the time, to introduce decorative elements into myriad architectural details. Island metalsmiths designed wall lights in the shape of fish for the clubhouse bar and bees to commemorate Bea Endicott Carstensen, an early Mill Reef homeowner. Local woodcrafters were brought onboard to fabricate draw pulls in the shapes of starfish, shells, and boats for built-in chests of drawers.

But it would be naive to suggest that Mill Reef is today totally unchanged from Ward's 1940s vision. It has morphed from a gathering place for sophisticated, primarily WASP adults looking to escape severe cold for long periods into a family resort where people come for relatively short stays, in many cases enjoying repeated visits between Thanksgiving and Easter that represent the Mill Reef season. The tradition of a July Fourth gathering has gained popularity in recent years, but, unlike some of its counterparts, such as Lyford Cay, which have become even less seasonal, Mill Reef has remained mainly a winter resort. The original Ward houses were small and not child-friendly. Adult friends and acquaintances were encouraged to visit (subject to the two-week rule for nonmembers), but they were expected to take rooms in the clubhouse. That particular vision has not become a legacy; in fact, it is difficult to fill the clubhouse except during the peak school-vacation periods over Christmas and spring break.

As the houses have expanded to include guest rooms, guesthouses, and swimming pools, Mill Reef has transitioned from a retreat for proprietary members and their adult friends to a gathering spot for members and their families. With that has come an em-

Friar's Head enjoys a landmark position on the east coast of the island as a non-operating lighthouse and sentinel for boats and ships.

The kidney-shaped dance floor at the Mill Reef clubhouse does double duty as a water catchment. A cistern is installed below it.

A cistern is ingeniously hidden in a masonry structure that resembles one of the windmills that dot the island.

Roof channels serve as catchments.

Ward encouraged local craftsmen to experiment with a variety of designs in local materials, including wood, shells, and concrete, which add a distinctive element of handcrafts and local folk art to houses such as Point of View, Signal Point, and Bamboo.

Pages 24 and 25:
View to the north, past Green Island, toward the outer reef that protects Nonsuch Bay. Fort Harman stands sentinel in the middle distance, and other Mill Reef houses dot the shoreline on the left.

phasis on sport—tennis, golf, and sailing—and the attendant growth of the yacht basin. Ward was an athlete, and the club has reflected his and others' interest in golf, sailing, gardening, tennis, croquet, and fishing. Today there is a greater emphasis on these activities, particularly as they relate to the family.

It is disturbing to contemplate what life would be like without Mill Reef: in it lives "the brief world of Far" that MacLeish longed to regain. Nothing compares to it. It is a place that values intellect and understatement. St. Bart's is glitzy. Who needs Hermes in the Caribbean? Overbuilding has occurred even on such obscure islands as Carriacou, Nevis, and St. Kitts. Select hotels on Antigua provide comfort and even a certain charm but also an unevenness resulting from poor town planning and indifferent architecture.

The changing times force us to reflect on the role of a club. Mill Reef faces challenges similar to those of the old summer resorts in the White Mountains of New Hampshire and Watch Hill, Rhode Island, where guests would arrive at grand hotels for the season with trunks and servants. Most of these businesses have either disappeared or become operations incorporating conventions, condominium units, or shared "cottages." Generational tastes change, and offspring who cannot afford their parents' lifestyle face the economic impossibility of running big houses with reduced means, no staff, and not enough vacation time. The financial survival of Mill Reef will depend on "new money" (or prudent "old money") from people who embrace and can afford Ward's vision of a utopian club for people from different geographic regions who share values, understatement, camaraderie, and congeniality, not to mention rum punch and the romance of "the brief world of Far." The legacy of Happy Ward is not related to family, large houses, instant communication, and technology's new developments at Mill Reef; nor does it relate to mass travel, exorbitant compensation packages, or casinos. His legacy is clearly social and architectural, influenced by a taste for the small scale, simplicity, diversity, and style. Like all art and architecture, these values demand stewardship.

The late Brendan Gill of the *New Yorker*, a noted preservationist, once wrote that "without a past we have no future." Although Mill Reef should not be frozen in a particular style or time, it must be respectful of its culture and heritage. How fortunate one is to be part of a place that provides not only recreation, escape, conviviality, sun, sea, and sky but also soul.

—Stephen S. Lash

1. "Shining Isles of the Caribbean," *Newsweek*, January 6, 1958: n.p.
2. Robertson Ward, autobiographical manuscript (Washington, D.C.: American Institute of Architects), 82.
3. Kathryn Livingston, "Antigua: Shimmering Shelter of the Elite," *Town & Country*, December 1976: 170–71.
4. "Shining Isles," op. cit.
5. Ted Patrick, "*Holiday* Invited You to Join a Crusade," *Holiday*, September 1946: n.p.
6. Ibid.
7. Archibald MacLeish, *This Music Crept by Me upon the Waters*, in *Six Plays* (Boston: Houghton Mifflin, 1980), 69–70.
8. Henry Fraser, Introduction, in *Architecture and Design in Barbados* (Canada: Keith Miller Publishing, 2001), 30.
9. R. H. Winnick, ed., *The Letters of Archibald MacLeish* (Boston: Houghton Mifflin, 1983), 354.
10. Ward designed about twenty-five modernist houses in New Canaan, Darien, and Greenwich, Connecticut. Among these was the first contemporary-style dwelling built in New Canaan and a Darien home for a Mr. Robins that was cited by *House and Garden* magazine in 1936 as one of six best houses in the nation.

Pages 28 and 29:
Distinctive masonry walls reflect the craftsmanship of the local stonemasons who quarried the outcroppings on which the Mill Reef clubhouse is built. The interior space is fitted with Ward's signature sophisticated stone archways in a modernist setting, including bold roof supports and an open exterior wall to the west.

Clubhouse (1949)

Happy Ward constructed the ten-room Mill Reef clubhouse before any houses so prospective members and guests would have a comfortable place to stay. "By the late summer of 1947 we began the difficult task of procuring our membership," he wrote in his autobiography, "but met with some success considering that virtually no one knew of that area of the West Indies and . . . upon hearing of Antigua, immediately assumed we were considering [another] Antigua, the ancient abandoned capital of Guatemala!" Ward asked top travel agents to send him their best customers. The Ward Room, an extension to the north, was added in 1981 using his designs. Andrew Goodenough oversaw an extensive remodeling of the rooms and cottages in the 1990s. He added suites to the triangular space that divided the original ten rooms from an additional set of rooms added later, combined rooms into larger areas, and designed additional cottages. The clubhouse has thirty-five rooms today.

The clubhouse entrance conveys a sense of theater. A passage through a garden court dominated by stately palms prepares the visitor for a panoramic view of the sea, framed by the sturdy lines of mid-century modern architecture. A low-slung arched roof deflects the wind.

A close-up of the school-of-fish chandelier designed by Ward's stepson, Amos Morrill, who worked on the Mill Reef clubhouse project from its inception.

The clubhouse bar and adjoining terrace are a favorite gathering place for visitors. It retains the original Morrill designs, including the chandelier and coral wall decoration.

In typical Ward fashion, a descent from the clubhouse provides an enticing vista of wind, sea, and sky.

Although the dining chairs are modern replacements, the core of this space remains unchanged, with its masonry tiles, handcrafted beams, and wall lights—all part of the original Mill Reef design.

Pages 36 and 37:
Past custom at the Mill Reef Club beach, on Exchange Bay, was to gather for a swim and rum punch at noon. But visitors today spend all day reading and napping under the cabanas, catching lunch at the nearby beach bar. The clubhouse and its bar are visible on the right.

CLUBHOUSE

1 guest room
2 barbecue pit
3 Ward Room
4 dining room
5 bar
6 parking
7 driveway
8 lobby
9 terrace
10 kitchen
11 dance floor/catchment
12 wine cellar
13 garden
14 commissary
15 administration offices
16 library/sitting room

This view of coconut palms outside the clubhouse golf course captures the spirited interplay of wind, sea, and sky at Mill Reef.

Bali Li (1950)

Happy Ward, whose vision and enterprise were key to the founding of Mill Reef, named his house Bali Li. This made-up name is derived from a collection of Balinese carvings he had purchased from a friend in Mexico City and installed in the house and from his siting of the structure in the lee of a hill to protect its garden from the wind. The house encircled a large inner courtyard where Ward, who was a serious orchid connoisseur and breeder, cultivated his plants. His other interests included competitive golf, sailing, and fishing, all of which he pursued at Mill Reef. He was born in 1897 in Florence, Italy, the out-of-wedlock son of a wealthy expatriate American art student from Cincinnati, Ohio, Helen Gordon Glenn, and the famed American sculptor Frederick William MacMonnies. He attended secondary school in New England and France and studied architecture at M.I.T. and Columbia University. He first visited the Caribbean in 1931 on a honeymoon cruise with his second wife, Dorothy Elliott Morrill. The peripatetic architect opened his practice in Boston in 1921 and lived in New York, New Canaan, Bermuda, and Mexico City before landing in Antigua in 1946. He later opened offices in the Bahamas, Barbados, London, and Sydney. Ward died in London in 1988, at age ninety.

A Balinese frieze, columns, and sculptures are integrated with Antiguan masonry, handcrafted wall lights, and a brise-soleil. The placement of a dining table on a stagelike rise epitomizes the theatricality found in Ward's work.

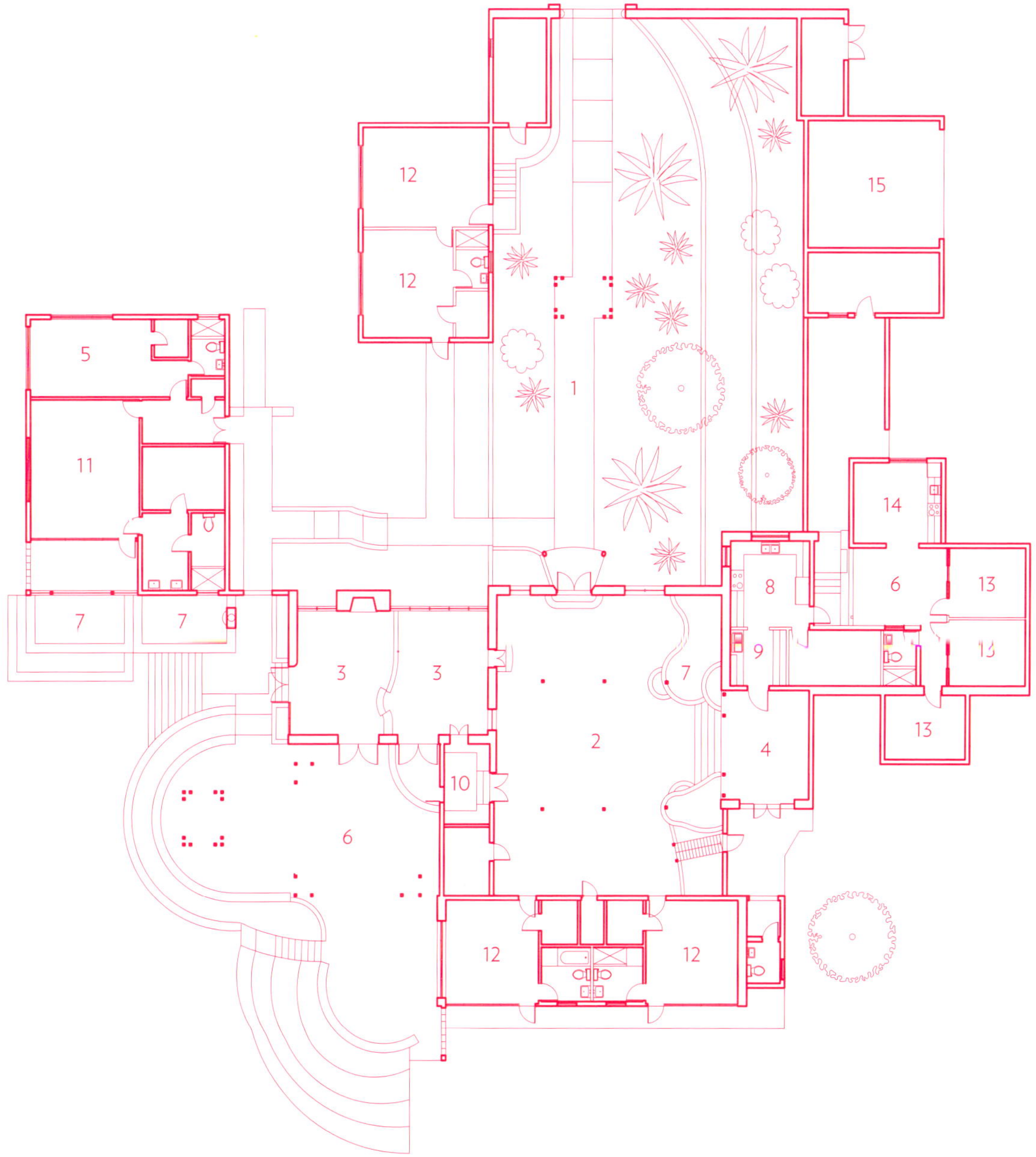

BALI LI

1 entrance
2 covered courtyard
3 living room
4 dining room
5 study
6 terrace
7 lily pond
8 kitchen
9 pantry
10 bar
11 master bedroom
12 guest bedroom
13 staff bedroom
14 service area
15 garage

The peaked red pergola at Bali Li shelters a former orchid court and entertaining space and abuts a raised dining room (see photo on page 39).

Bali Li's entrance wall is topped with a series of terraced ziggurats, pyramidal structures that originated in ancient Mesopotamian temples. The massive carved stones lend a note of dignity to a fairy-tale edifice.

Antiguan craftsmanship includes masonry skills coupled with innovative metalwork and the use of cinder block, which is often perforated with various designs.

The seaside terrace at Bali Li faces Exchange Bay. Andrew Goodenough's 1995 pergola extends Ward's covered outdoor terrace.

Ward selected this site for his own house, Bali Li, where he lived until 1965.

Fort Harman (1950)

One of fifty-one fortifications built during the seventeenth and eighteenth centuries to protect the British sugar trade on Antigua, Fort Harman commanded the main channel leading to Nonsuch Bay, opposite Green Island. Ward's close friends Bertram and Polly Work, American residents of Bermuda who accompanied the architect on his exploration in 1946 of the area that would become Mill Reef, built a two-bedroom house on the property, where they lived during construction of a house on the fortifications. Bert Work was interested in aviation and helped to train Royal Air Force pilots in Bermuda during World War II. Fort Harman is associated with Sir John Harman (1625–1673), a distinguished British admiral who served in the eastern Caribbean. It is also linked in land records to heirs of Samuel Harman, who in the nineteenth century owned the land on which the fort stands.

The range of building sites on the inlets and promontories of the eastern shore of Antigua appealed to early Mill Reef Club members such as Bert and Polly Work. Fort Harman is a magnificent house site, with water on three sides and protected by shallow reefs.

There is theater in the approach to many of Ward's houses at Mill Reef, whether through a garden walk or an interior flight of stairs.

Wrought-iron furniture from the 1950s survives at Fort Harman, as it does at other Mill Reef houses, reflecting the taste of that period.

FORT HARMAN

1 entrance hall
2 living room
3 outdoor sitting room
4 dining room
5 terrace
6 pool
7 kitchen
8 pantry
9 bar
10 master bedroom
11 guest bedroom

The combination of the tray ceiling, complete with moldings, recesses, and furniture arrangements, brings Park Avenue to the tropics. The masonry wall pierced by the small window utilizes a former British gun embrasure.

These nine-pound guns were aimed toward Green Island to guard the main channel leading to Nonsuch Bay, a popular destination for Mill Reef Club guests and yachtsmen.

Ward added this saltwater pool in 1984. It is bordered by thumb pots from Sea View Farms, on Antigua.

Friar's Head (1952)

Named for the promontory on which it sits, this house was constructed for John Cowles (1898–1983), a newspaper and magazine publisher from Des Moines and Minneapolis. Its cupola is a familiar landmark—resembling a lighthouse—visible throughout Mill Reef, and the house is noted on nautical charts. Cowles, a 1921 Harvard graduate and longtime overseer of the university, had wide-ranging interests in politics, foreign policy, education, and the arts. "Building a house at Mill Reef is the most fantastically foolish thing that Betty and I have done in 28 years of marriage," he wrote to his family, "but we both want to do it." Friar's Head is the most exposed house at Mill Reef, unprotected by offshore islands from Atlantic storms and gales. Two cottages were added in 1960 and 1999.

Friar's Head, also named on old maps of Antigua as Frye Head and Friars Head, provides a magnificent house setting. Note the basic modular structure, united by a cruciform plan and signaled by a sentinel palm.

The approach to Friar's Head is understated but dramatic.

Friar's Head seen from the land is a very private site in a windy landscape.

FRIAR'S HEAD

1 entrance hall
2 living room
3 sitting room
4 dining room
5 terrace
6 kitchen
7 pantry
8 bar
9 master bedroom
10 guest bedroom
11 staff bedroom
12 service area
13 garage
14 cupola

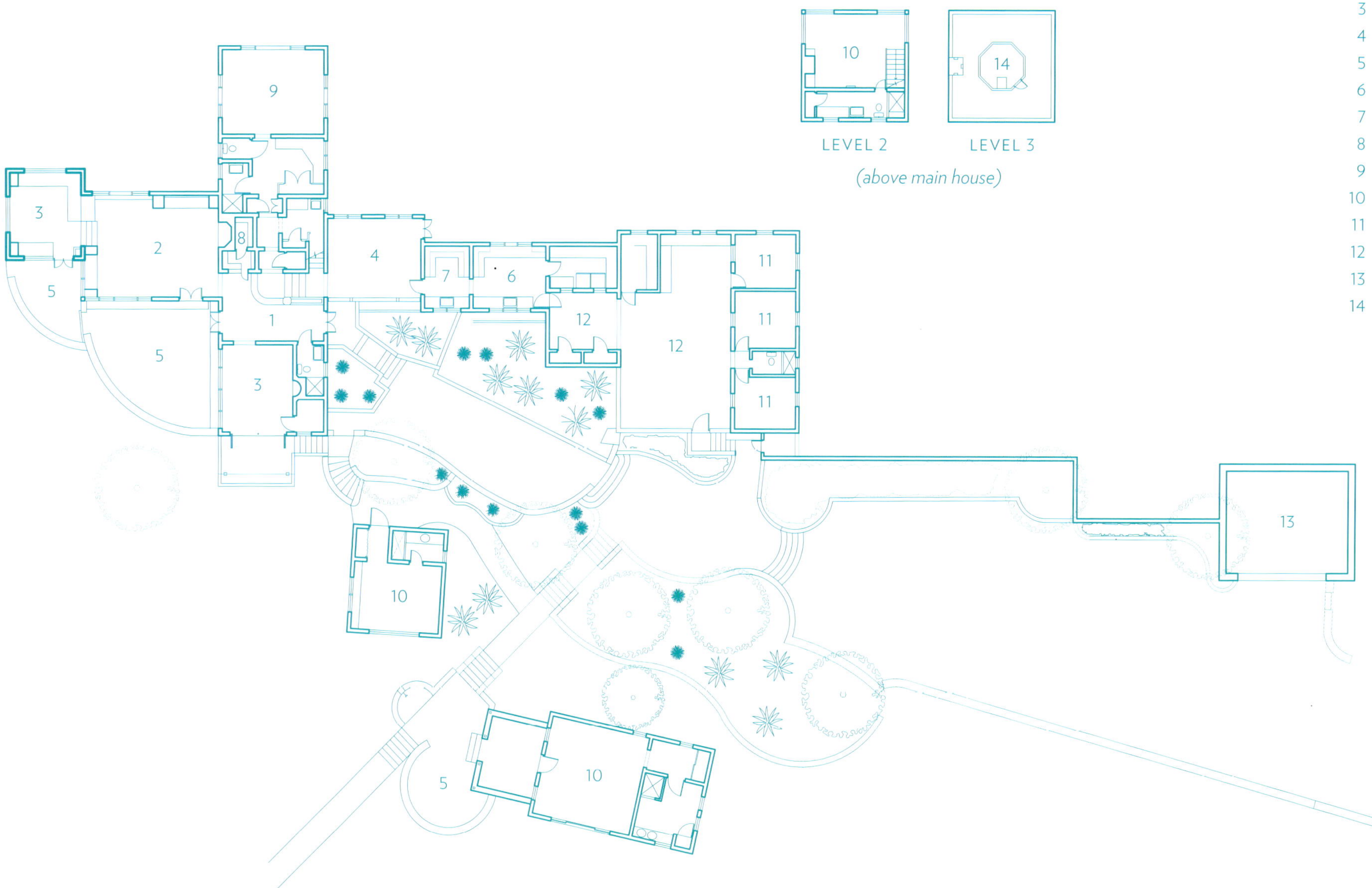

This porch at Friar's Head is a later addition, framing a view of the reconstructed Archibald MacLeish house, situated directly across Marigalante Bay.

The juxtaposition of these two doorways provides a surreal Magritte-like quality to outside and inside doors at Friar's Head.

This living room was constructed to withstand Atlantic storms. Note the bold reinforcing curved beam and the built-in furniture around the perimeter of the room.

AMERICAN HERITAGE
dic·tion·ar·y

Signal Point (1953)

Marjorie Fleming Lloyd-Smith, heiress to a West Coast lumber fortune, had this modernist house built on a dramatic point between the clubhouse beach on Exchange Bay and Half Moon Bay. In 1926, her father, Arthur Henry Fleming, of Pasadena, California, acquired the French railroad car in which the armstice ending World War I had been signed and donated it to the French government. In 1940, Adolf Hitler forced France to sign its humiliating capitulation to Germany in the same railroad car. Marjorie's first husband, Wilton Lloyd-Smith (1894–1940), was the scion of a New York state legal dynasty, a big-game hunter, and a consummate "clubman." The couple had four daughters, one of whom, Marne Lloyd-Smith Hornblower, inherited the house. Marjorie married Knight Woolley (1896–1980), a Yale Bonesman and distinguished partner in the Wall Street private bank Brown Brothers Harriman, in 1957 in St. Philip's Anglican Church, a few miles from Mill Reef.

Ward planted Signal Point comfortably on a point of land between Half Moon Bay and Exchange Bay. The beach hut once had charming mural decorations by Amos Morrill that have since been washed away by hurricanes.

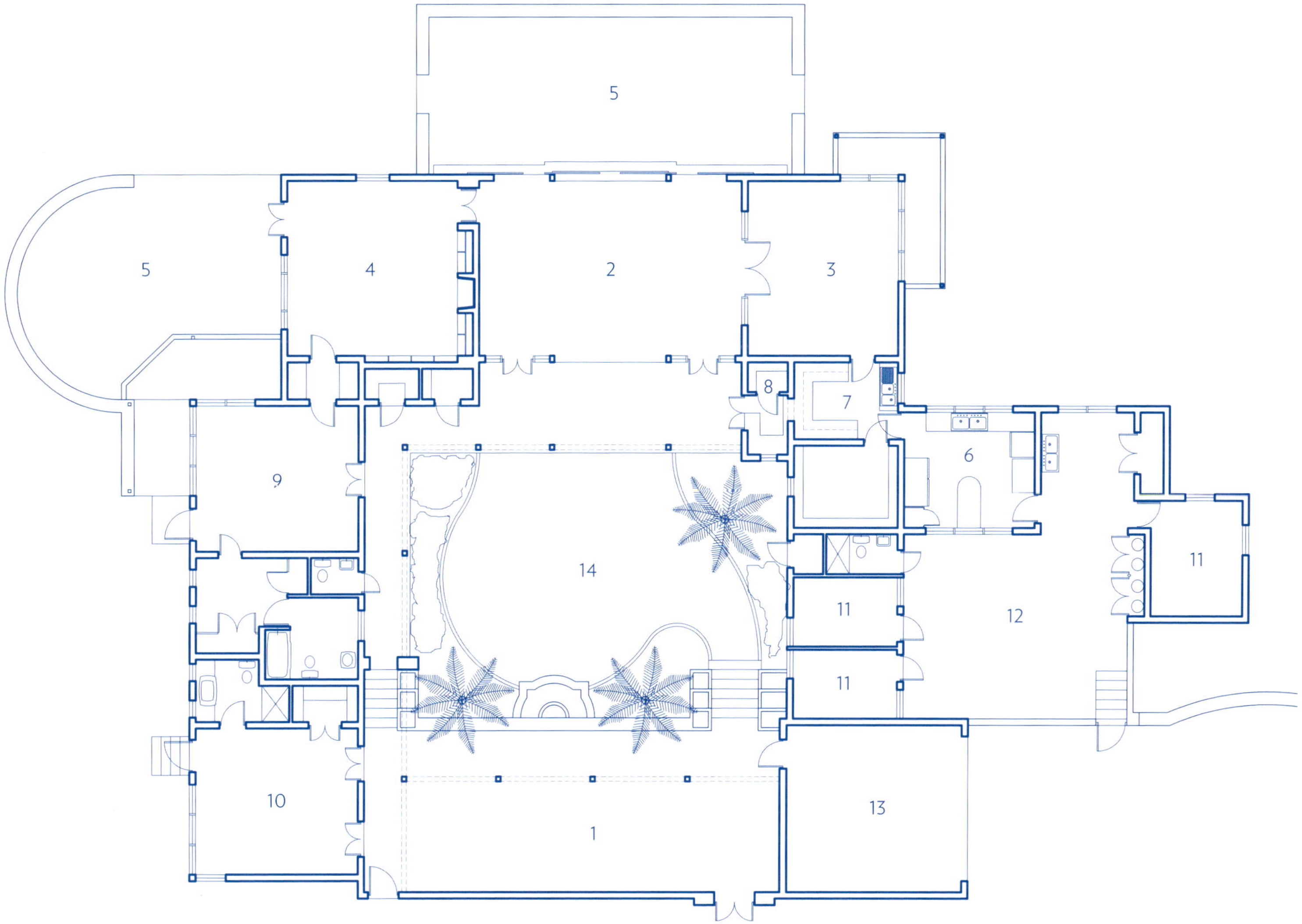

SIGNAL POINT

1 entrance/indoor garden
2 living room
3 dining room
4 study
5 terrace
6 kitchen
7 pantry
8 bar
9 master bedroom
10 guest bedroom
11 staff bedroom
12 service area
13 garage
14 patio

The blazing sun beats down on the unprotected terrace of Signal Point, with its view across Exchange Bay to Bali Li and Friar's Head.

The formal entrance with broken pediments surmounted by a pineapple, the traditional symbol of hospitality, opens to a outdoor garden through which one enters the house.

This patio, which conceals a water catchment and cistern, leads to a small seating area. It serves as a passage from the garden to the living room.

The Signal Point garden room provides shelter from the sun with a charming play of light and shadow.

Elaborate built-in furniture is a typical feature of mid-century modern style.

Pages 72 and 73:
This dramatic view of the sunset over Exchange Bay from Bali Li shows the Mill Reef clubhouse and cottages on the right and Signal Point on the left.

These close-ups highlight the craftsmanship that accompanied the construction of Ward's Mill Reef houses.

The library at Signal Point seems the sort of space one might associate more with a New York apartment than with a retreat in the Leeward Islands.

Pages 76 and 77:
Aquamarine demonstrates the crisp modernist architecture and garden design of Happy Ward. The seamless addition of an expanded master suite was designed by Amos Morrill in the 1980s.

Aquamarine (1950s)

This modernist house was built for the financier William E. Hutton, a second cousin of the legendary banker E. F. Hutton. His wife was Joan King Chapin, daughter of Detroit automobile magnate and U.S. Secretary of Commerce Roy D. Chapin. Joan was a skilled photographer, amateur pilot, competitive swimmer, and renowned hostess. The Huttons' living room at Aquamarine had a large aquarium wall, and the dining room was painted a deep blue to evoke the marine life beneath the waves. Its vast living room, in the shape of an expanded "U," opening to the sea, is one of the largest rooms at Mill Reef. It reflects a Frank Lloyd Wrightian ideal of organic spaces. The Huttons also owned a mansion on Long Island, built by the celebrated architect John Russell Pope. It is today part of the C. W. Post campus of Long Island University.

The beach houses along Great Deep and Little Deep bays epitomize Ward's ability to create elegant designs submerged in a stunning landscape.

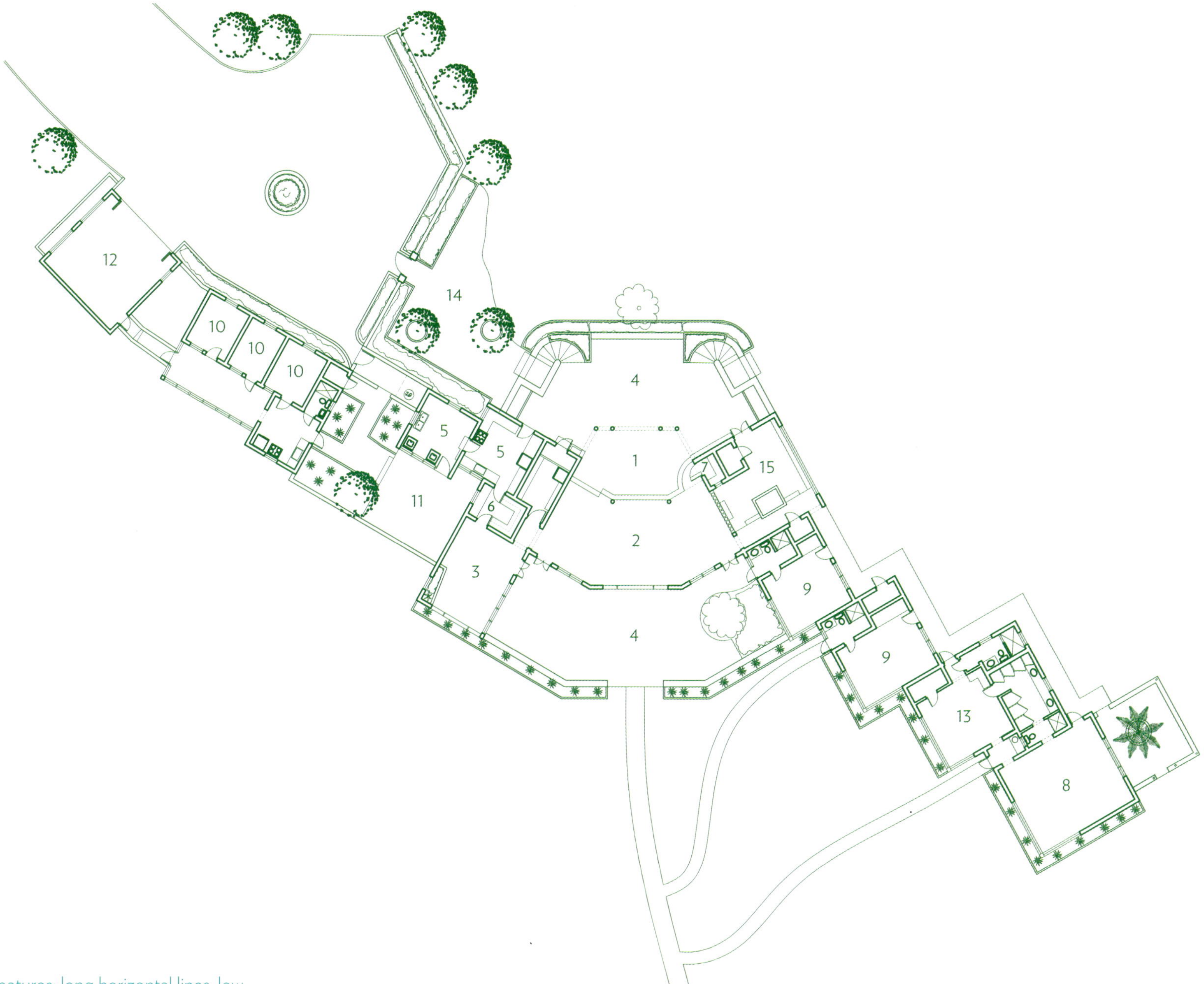

AQUAMARINE

1 entrance hall
2 living room
3 dining room
4 terrace
5 kitchen
6 pantry
7 bar
8 master bedroom
9 guest bedroom
10 staff bedroom
11 service area
12 garage
13 lounge
14 courtyard
15 indoor plant room

The beach houses share many features: long horizontal lines, low roofs, and rooms that are open to the west and often face a croquet court. These are the most sought-after locations at Mill Reef—sometimes referred to as its gold coast.

Marine life is the decorative theme at Aquamarine. These
wall appliqués were crafted by local metalworkers.

This photo shows one of the seating areas in the large Aquamarine living room.
The bamboo screen of today replaces the original large aquarium.
Note two classic Ward features: a walk-in bar to the left
and an indoor plant room to the right.

This perforated cinder-block wall and entrance gate, partly concealed by the circular planter, are reminiscent of Ward's early work in Bermuda.

The spacious living room, which opens directly onto a cleared field that was once a croquet court, demonstrates the lack of a need for west-facing walls in Ward's Mill Reef houses. This dramatic room has a coffered ceiling and classical supporting columns that originally framed a terrazzo dance floor.

Bamboo (1956)

Elsa Mott Mitchell Ives (1903–1988), a General Motors heiress, and her first husband, Hamish Mitchell, a Scottish GM executive and wartime Royal Air Force officer, lived in Bermuda and were close friends of Happy Ward. Sharing his vision for Mill Reef, they purchased their lot in 1947. Bamboo was one of a series of low, horizontal houses built along the sweep of Great Deep Bay that owe much to Frank Lloyd Wright. The slat areas, roof shape and overhangs, ceiling framing, built-in banquettes, and floor design all evoke Taliesin West. A celebrated wit and hostess, Elsa often invited friends for moonlight dinner and dancing, followed by skinny-dipping. In 1957, she married Kenneth Appelton Ives, a Yale graduate, real estate developer, and member of the winning U.S. crew team at the 1924 Paris Olympics.

This classic Mill Reef house has benefited from particularly attentive stewardship by its present owner. Note the curved sloping ceiling, which is broken by a latticed roof that allows rain to fall on the indoor plants and fish pond. The dining room table comprises a glass top set upon a cement composition of reef encrusted with shells and coral.

Pages 88 and 89:
Bamboo paneling survives the test of time and testifies to Ward's resourcefulness. The bamboo supports, filled with concrete and insect repellent, hold the roof down, not up! Elsa Mott Mitchell Ives's sister Susan Mott Webb later purchased a house on Exchange Bay.

BAMBOO

1 living room
2 dining room
3 terrace
4 fish pond
5 kitchen
6 pantry
7 bar
8 master bedroom
9 guest bedroom
10 staff bedroom
11 service area
12 garage
13 plant room

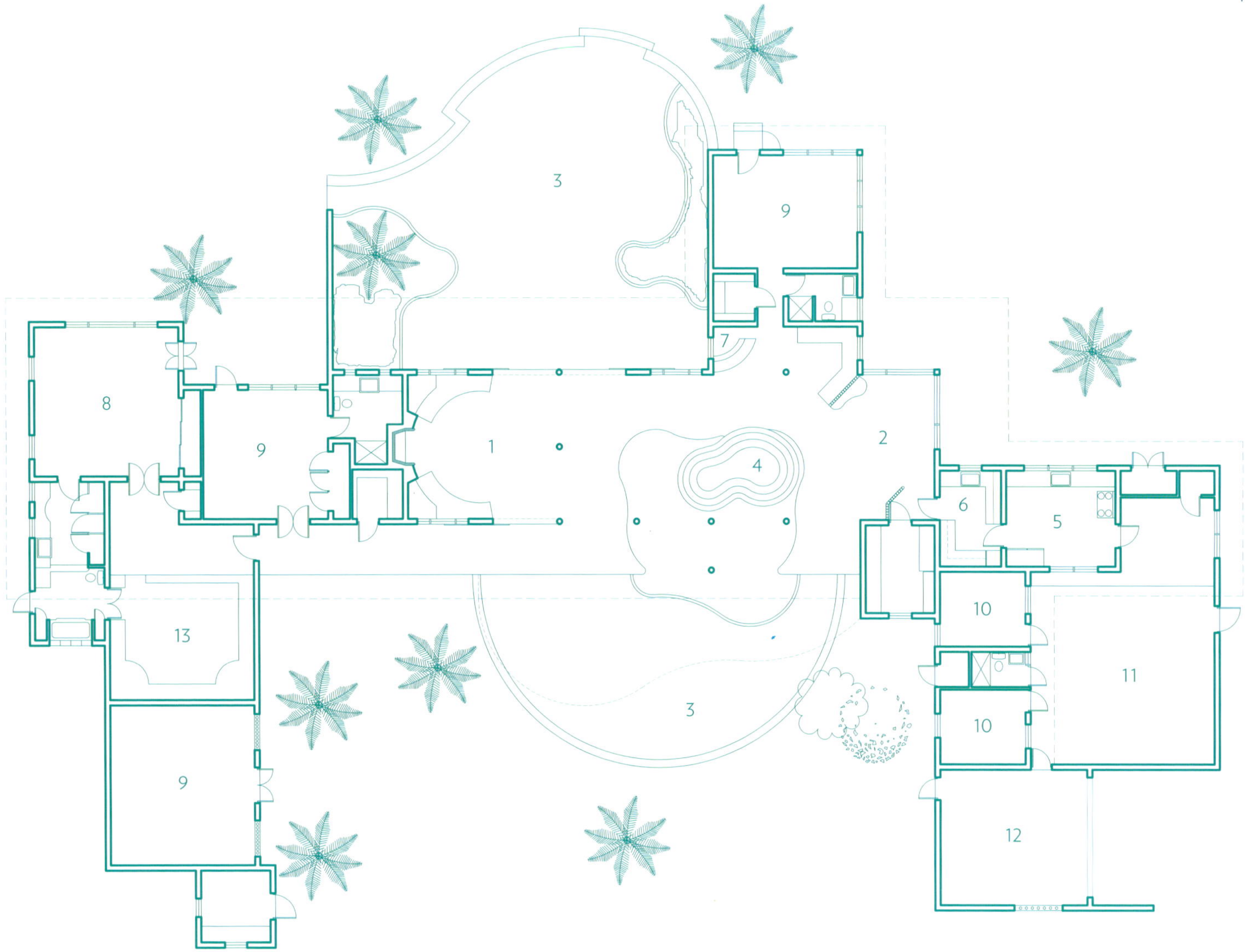

Bamboo nestles comfortably in a parklike setting connected with, but not dominating, an adjacent expanse of beach.

Hollywood hits the tropics in the glamorous bedroom commissioned by General Motors heiress Elsa Mott Mitchell Ives. (Her half-brother Stewart Mott was a celebrated New York philanthropist, political activist, and truck-farmer who operated out of his Park Avenue penthouse.) Note the fitted furniture, pickled-wood ceiling, seashell drawer pulls, dressing table, and mirrors.

Point of View (1950s)

Perched above the clubhouse, Point of View is today a popular rental house. It was built for the New York investment banker Mason B. Starring II (b. 1889). Starring's son Mason (Buzz) III, an early OSS and CIA officer who inherited the house and became Mill Reef Club president, was awarded the Croix de Guerre for heroism behind enemy lines in World War II. A partner in the Wall Street investment firm Dominick & Dominick, he married Nancy Donaldson, a granddaughter of Coleman du Pont, in 1947. Nancy was an accomplished landscape architect, tennis player, and pianist who produced a book on the trees of Mill Reef. The house was updated in 1999 with the expansion of terraces and rooms and the building of a freshwater swimming pool and pool house—all by Andrew Goodenough. The addition of the pool was possible only because the Antiguan government had recently begun delivering water to Mill Reef from its desalination plant in St. John's.

Point of View is an example of a house that has retained its original design while being updated and enlarged by Andrew Goodenough. Old and new are combined with an abundance of chamfered columns and open rooms.

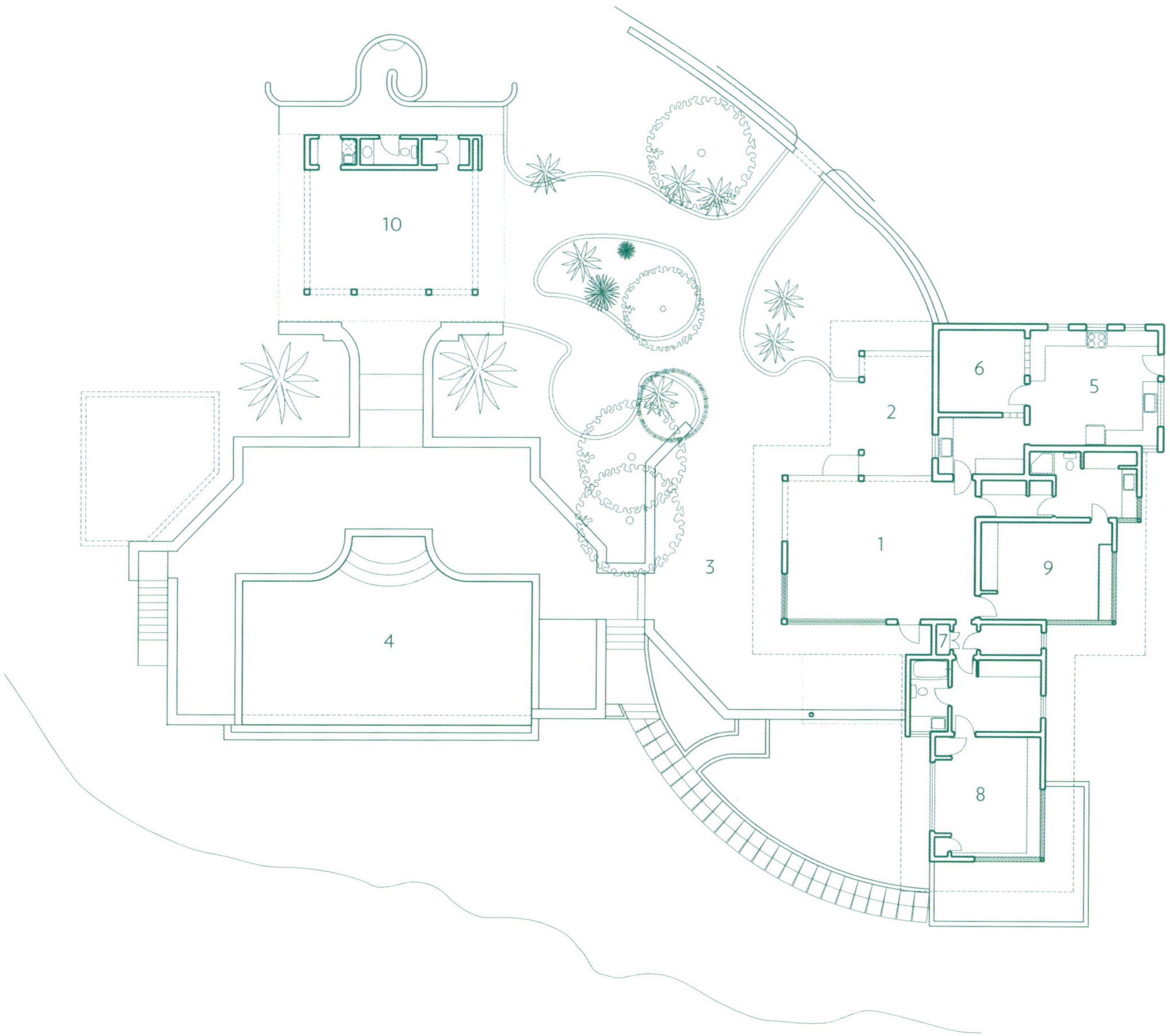

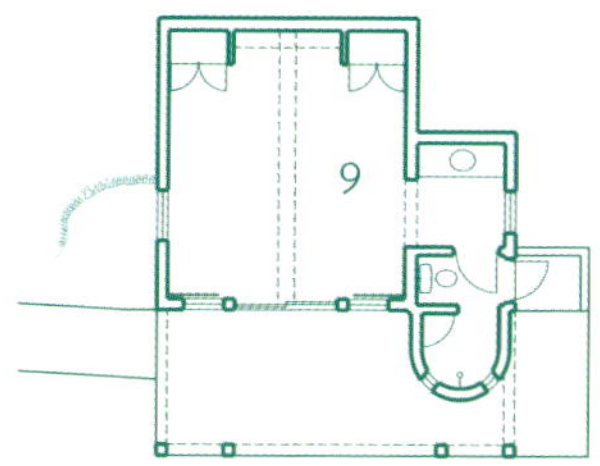

LEVEL 1 *(below main house)*

POINT OF VIEW

1 entrance/living room
2 dining room
3 terrace
4 pool
5 kitchen
6 pantry
7 bar
8 master bedroom
9 guest bedroom
10 pool house

The living room looks out to a new pool pavilion and an arched entrance, recent additions done in the spirit of Happy Ward.

A rolling savanna is visible though abutting windows under a low-slung roof. The pattern of pickled-wood beams in geometic shapes and a variety of materials appears in many of Ward's ceilings.

A recently added brise-soleil on an extended terrace unites the mid-century modern with the architecture of today. The sturdy geometric roof supports a highly vulnerable yet stunning windswept setting.

Ward experimented with materials such as cinder block, which provides a decorative feature and evokes stylistic elements found in south Florida modernist architecture of the 1950s.

The house's connection with sea, sky, clouds, and palms is amplified by Andrew Goodenough's addition of a disappearing-edge pool.

Moongate (1950s)

The moon gate, a traditional Chinese garden element, is a circular opening in a wall through which people walk. It often is associated with a transition from the ordinary world of humans to the natural world and a moment of spiritual renewal. Moongate was the name given to his Mill Reef house by M. Douglas Lawrence, son of the New York real estate developer who donated the land in Bronxville, New York, where Sarah Lawrence College was built. Lawrence commissioned many Asian features, including a moon gate, in this residence, which is perched high on a volcanic mound between Great and Little Deep bays. As Mill Reef Club president, Lawrence sought publicity in selected magazines to promote the club and attract more members. A photo spread in the January 4, 1960, issue of *Sports Illustrated* featured Mrs. Lawrence and other members, in dignified bathing suits and sporting attire, fishing, swimming, and playing croquet "in the perfect place in the sun." Andrew Goodenough extensively expanded the house starting in 1994, adding more moon gates and taking advantage of its dramatic views.

The attractive but subdued entrance to Moongate gives a glimpse of the sea beyond but leaves the visitor unprepared for the drama of the site and the exotic architecture.

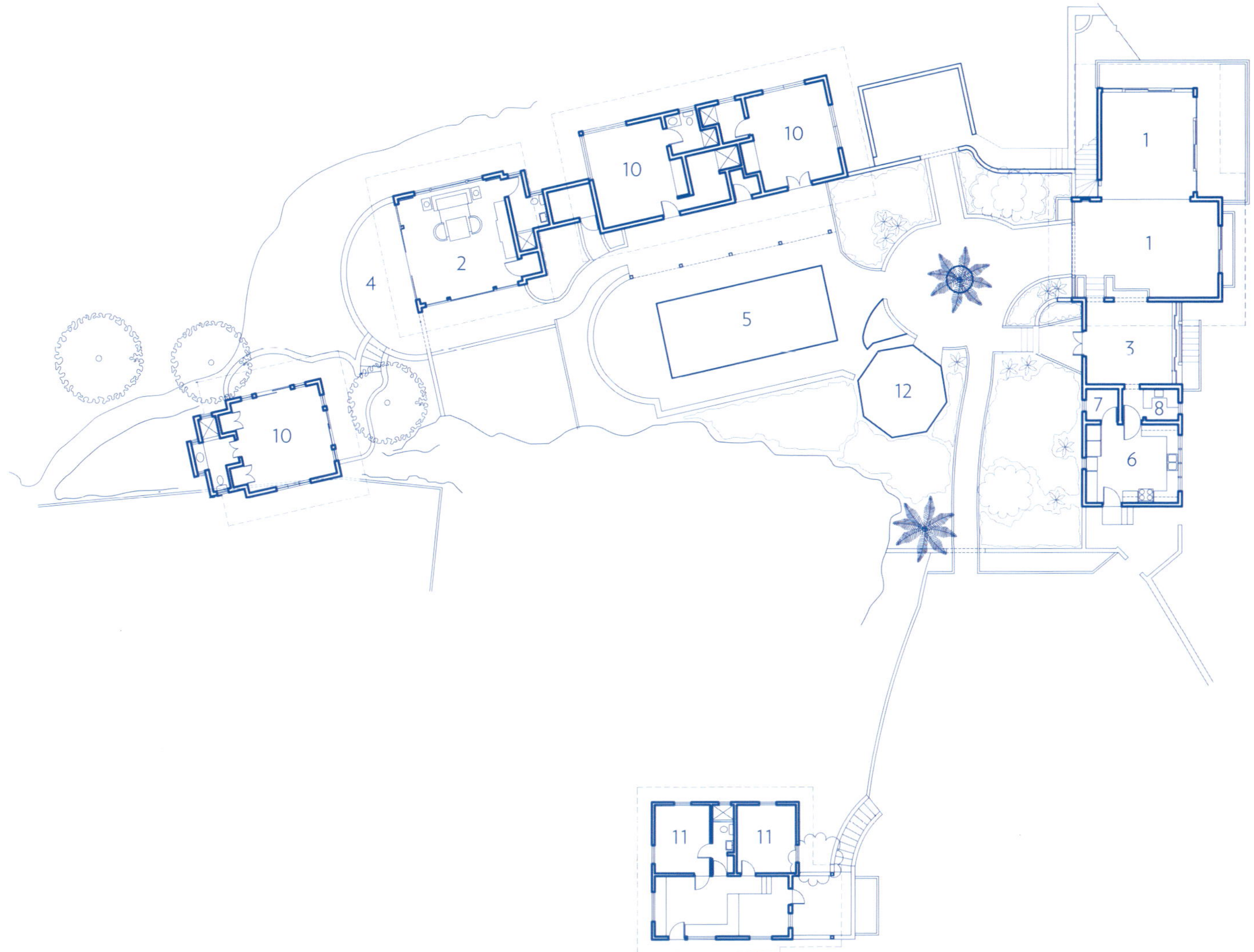

MOONGATE

1 entrance hall/living room
2 sitting room
3 dining room
4 terrace
5 pool
6 kitchen
7 pantry
8 bar
9 master bedroom
10 guest bedroom
11 staff bedroom
12 gazebo

LEVEL 1
(below main house)

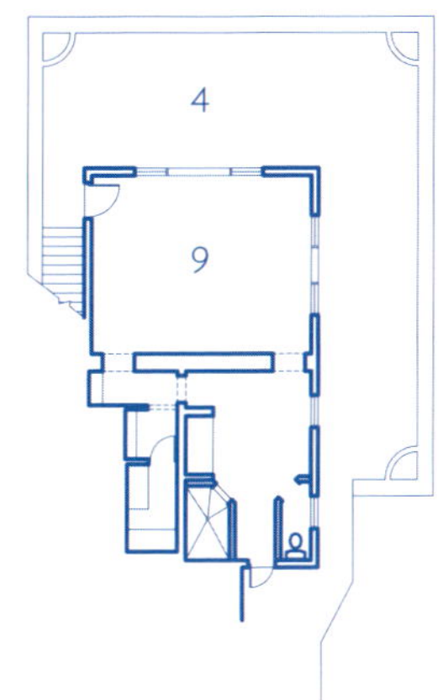

This master bedroom, its terrace decorated with cannons found elsewhere on the island, was added by Andrew Goodenough.

Drawer pulls at Moongate reinforce the Chinese theme, as does the Ward gate, which frames a classic Antiguan view.

Moongate evokes the Chinese-style village designed by Henry Killam Murphy in Coral Gables, Florida, in 1926.

Pages 108 and 109:
Rain clouds build up over York Island.

This is a view toward Neck of Land from Moongate.

The living room expansion by Andrew Goodenough takes advantage of the sweeping views at the site and extends the coffered ceiling Ward designed.

Onesuch (1958)

This house was built for Laurens Hammond (1895–1973), the Chicago engineer, inventor, and sailor who invented the Hammond organ. It is situated on a steep hill on Nonsuch Bay, where Hammond built a dock for his sailboat. His daughter Lisa married Desmond Nicholson (1925–2006), a local historian and a founder of Nicholson Yacht Charters at English Harbour. The Nicholson family arrived on Antigua by sailboat in 1949, the same year Mill Reef was launched. Club members like Hammond often chartered the Nicholsons' seventy-foot schooner, *Mollihawk*, and took a keen interest in the development of both the charter company and restoration of the fortifications at English Harbour.

The Georgian fretwork of the Onesuch balcony reflects Ward's evolution from a modernist and eclectic aesthetic to the embrace of a more traditional style.

ONESUCH

1 entrance hall
2 living room
3 sitting room
4 dining room
5 terrace
6 kitchen
7 pantry
8 bar
9 master bedroom
10 guest bedroom
11 staff bedroom
12 service area
13 garage
14 courtyard
15 lily pond/fountain
16 indoor plant room
17 cistern

The plan of Onesuch confirms Ward's reliance on a garden entrance with descending stairways, exterior corridors with masonry archways, and the incorporation of indoor/outdoor spaces.

Ward was particularly skilled at guiding the visitor through a series of paths and corridors punctuated by arches and steps.

Bars are integral to all Mill Reef houses, each boasting its own variety of rum punch.

REEF CLUB

Antiguan folk art resurfaces in the metalwork of Lorne Maxim, son of Denfield Maxim, who made the tin lights at the Mill Reef clubhouse.

A similar design to the clubhouse, but revisited a decade later, presents a sophisticated structure on Nonsuch Bay. It brings together many familiar Ward features. The house's massive walls lend a sense of security to its location at the bottom of a steep hill.

Isiri (1962)

The series of buildings cascading down the promontory on Conch Point and its Georgian boathouse are iconic Mill Reef structures overlooking Nonesuch Bay and Green Island. The house was built for J. Noel Macy (1900–1977), a newspaper publisher and army officer who served in the War Department's Bureau of Public Relations and, later, the Department of State. He was a descendant of Thomas Macy, a whaling captain and original Nantucket Island settler. The Macy family founded an oil company that was sold to Standard Oil, and they became benefactors of Columbia University. In 1945, Noel married his third wife, Elena Aldcroftt Kohler, of New York, a wartime colleague who had served with the Red Cross and OSS in Northern Ireland, Africa, and the Middle East. An avid sailor, Macy led many cruises for Mill Reef Club members on his famous eighty-six-foot 1907 schooner, *Freelance*. The property was inherited by his son, A. Martin Macy (1926–1996), a Virginia aviation executive, and his wife, Bona Comel di Socebran, and remains in the family today.

A mature Ward created a sophisticated design with the addition of a shingle kick roof, marking a step toward gentrification and a changed environment from the corrugated metal of Mill Reef's earlier days. Isiri, which follows the plan of an eighteenth-century plantation house, consists of a series of structures with shingle roofs.

In the Arawak language, Isiri means "point of land." This house, among the most sophisticated at Mill Reef, reflects classical order and evokes Antigua's British colonial history.

When Isiri was built in 1962, it featured Mill Reef's first private pool. It is filled with saltwater and has a disappearing edge.

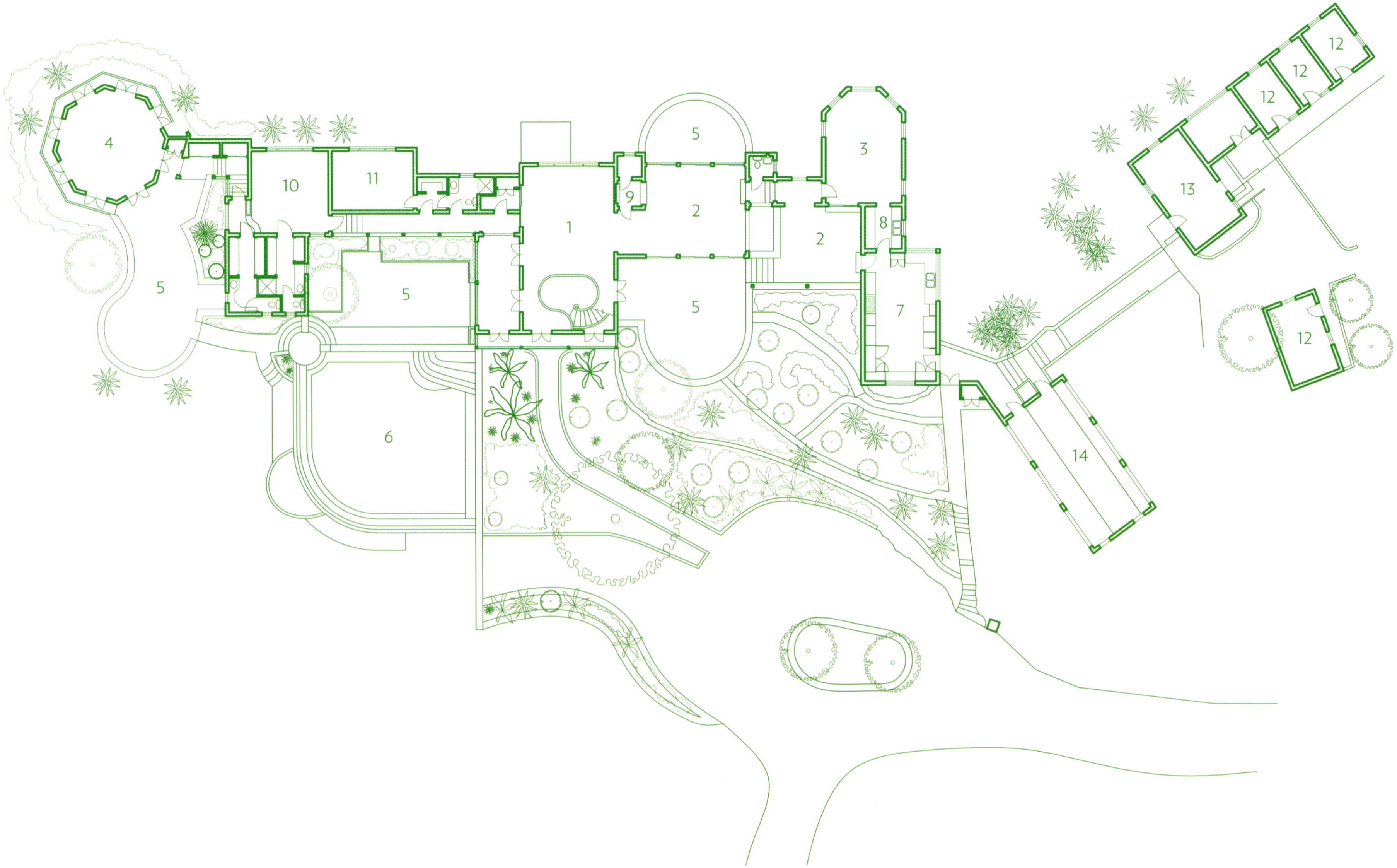

ISIRI

1 living room
2 sitting room
3 dining room
4 library
5 terrace
6 pool
7 kitchen
8 pantry
9 bar
10 master bedroom
11 guest bedroom
12 staff bedroom
13 service area
14 greenhouse

The comfortable sitting room at Isiri opens, on one side, through a classical loggia onto an interior garden and, behind the viewer, through glass doors onto a seaside terrace (see photo, page 119).

The boathouse at Isiri includes guest accommodations and features an elegant Chippendale exterior balustrade.

The octagonal library at Isiri, modeled after an Arawak hut, reflects the influence of resort developments such as Round Hill in Jamaica, which opened in 1954.

Selected Works of Robertson Ward

Ward opened his practice in Boston in 1921. From that year until 1927, the firm name was Robertson Ward, Architect; from 1927 to 1941, it was Robertson Ward, Architect, A.I.A. He established a Caribbean practice on Antigua in 1947. The firm of Robertson Ward Associates, Architects, St. John's, Antigua, was founded in 1956, when James C. Walker became a partner. Other partners and office locations followed, in Nassau (1958), Barbados (1960), London (1965), Sydney (1971), Trinidad (1976), and Grand Cayman (1982). The firm continues today as Robertson Ward Associates International, Ltd. (RWA), with offices on Antigua and Barbados and in the Bahamas.

1923 • Falmouth Junior High School, Falmouth, Mass.

1925 • Harry Apthorp house, Boston

1932 • Philip Wagoner house, Ridgefield, Conn.

1935 • Russell Pettingill houses, 148–152 East 38th Street, New York (redesign of a nineteenth-century farmhouse)
• Velma B. Woolworth Memorial Chapel, Woodlawn Cemetery, New York

1937 • Franklin B. Kirkbride house, New Canaan, Conn.

1939 • Frances Drake house, Paget, Bermuda
• William Greve house, Long Bird Island, Bermuda
• Duncan MacMartin house, Pembroke, Bermuda

1940 • Consulting architect, U.S. Army, Kindley Field, Bermuda

1944 • Hotel de las Americas, Acapulco

1945 • Alberto Pullen house, Acapulco

1949 • Mill Reef clubhouse, Antigua

1950 • Bali Li (Robertson Ward house), Mill Reef Club, Antigua
• Fort Harman (Bertram Work house), Mill Reef Club, Antigua

1952 • Friar's Head (John Cowles house), Mill Reef Club, Antigua

1953 • Signal Point (Marjorie Fleming Lloyd-Smith house), Mill Reef Club, Antigua

1954 • Estate Carleton Resort, St. Croix, U.S. Virgin Islands

1955 • Admiral's Inn, Nelson's Dockyard, English Harbour, Antigua (restoration)
• Half Moon Bay Hotel, Antigua

1956 • Bamboo (Elsa Mott Mitchell Ives house), Mill Reef Club, Antigua

1958 • William Holden house, Mustique, St. Vincent and the Grenadines
• Antigua Horizons Hotel, Antigua
• Curtain Bluff Hotel, Antigua
• Onesuch (Laurens Hammond house), Mill Reef Club, Antigua

1959 • Air terminal building, St. John's, Antigua

1960 • Villa Contenta (William Simpson house), Lyford Cay Club, Nassau, Bahamas
• Juan Trippe house, Cotton Bay Club, Eleuthera, Bahamas

1961 • Arthur Vining Davis house, Cotton Bay Club, Eleuthera, Bahamas
• Round the Bend (Sir Gerritt van der Woude house), Lyford Cay Club, Nassau, Bahamas

1962 • Henry Breck, Lord Kindersley house, Barbados
• Isiri (J. Noel Macy house), Mill Reef Club, Antigua
• Sandy Lane, Barbados

1963 • Pytchley Lodge (Sir Gerald Glover house), Lyford Cay Club, Nassau, Bahamas
• Robert Trent Jones house, Cotton Bay Club, Eleuthera, Bahamas

1964 • La Tourelle (Robertson Ward house), Milly-la-Forêt, France

1966 • Settler's Beach development, Barbados

1967 • Ingrid Bergman house, Choiseul, France
• San Souci condominiums, Ochos Rios, Jamaica

1968 • Cobbler's Cove Hotel, Barbados
• Golf du Bercuit resort and golf course, near Brussels

1969 • Aquarius (Robertson Ward house), Barbados
• John A. McCone house, Cotton Bay Club, Eleuthera, Bahamas

1970 • Lord Bernstein house, Barbados
• Edgar Kaiser house, Cotton Bay Club, Eleuthera, Bahamas
• Holiday Inns, St. Lucia and Grenada
• La Toc Hotel, St. Lucia
• Cariblue Hotel, St. Lucia

1971 • Sandpiper Inn, Barbados

1975 • Heywood Holiday Village Hotel, Barbados

1976 • 22 Wilton Street, London (Robertson Ward townhouse; remodeled interiors)

1977 • Jose Loreto Arismendi house, Caracas

A sunset view from Bali Li over Smith Island and Soldier's Point, across Exchange and Half Moon bays

ELIZABETH BALLANTINE is a lawyer and journalist based in McLean, Virginia. She holds a B.A. and Ph.D. in history from Yale University and a J.D. from American University in Washington, D.C. She is a director of two newspaper companies and a trustee of both Grinnell College and the American University of Paris. Her grandfather John Cowles built the house at Mill Reef called Friar's Head in 1952. It remains in the family today.

RICHARD CHEEK, one of the country's foremost architectural photographers, has been recording the visual history of American architecture and landscape design since 1966 for books that serve scholarly and popular audiences alike. The author of fourteen photographic books on the nation's historic buildings and landscapes, he has also provided illustrations for more than seventy architectural histories and guides. As a collector of American architectural books and ephemera and a bibliographic consultant, he helped initiate Historic New England's new publications series and serves as its editor.

STEPHEN S. LASH is chairman emeritus of Christie's in North and South America. Born and raised in Boston, he holds B.A. and M.B.A. degrees from Yale and Columbia universities. Currently, he serves on the boards of several preservation organizations. He lives in New York and Stonington, Connecticut, with his wife, Wendy Lehman Lash, with whom he honeymooned at Mill Reef in 1967.

Half-title page:
The elegant entrance to the garden at Exchange Place leads from the outdoors to another dramatic outdoors view across Exchange Bay, with Smith Island in the distance. The obelisk rises above a circular pond, fed by a cascading double fountain.

Frontispiece:
The view from Friar's Head across Marigalante Bay.

Published by The Derrydale Press
An imprint of The Rowman & Littlefield Publishing Group, Inc.
4501 Forbes Boulevard, Suite 200, Lanham, MD 20706
www.rlpgtrade.com
Estover Road, Plymouth PL6 7PY, United Kingdom

Distributed by National Book Network

Text © 2011 Elizabeth Ballantine and Stephen S. Lash
Photographs © 2011 Richard Cheek

All rights reserved. No part of this book may be reproduced in any form or by any electronic or mechanical means, including information storage and retrieval systems, without written permission from the publisher, except for passages quoted in reviews .

British Library Cataloguing-in-Publication Information available

ISBN 978-1-58667-125-9

Book and jacket design by Julia Sedykh Design
House plans by Andrew Goodenough
Printed and bound in China by C&C Offset Printing Co., Ltd.